My Brutha:

Surviving the System

JERMAINE DUNHAM

Book cover designed by Reel Designs
Memoir edited by Olivia Shaw-Reel

ISBN: 979-8-9854332-0-3

Dedication

To Prince – Innocent & Light
My son, you have just begun…

To My Bruthas & Sistas –
We are all connected and a part of each other. Use your failures to elevate. It's a process worth gaining.

Eternal light & love,

-Jermaine

"I have said these things to you, that in Me you may have peace. In the world you will have tribulation. But take heart; I have overcome the world."

-John 16:33

1 | *Straight, No Chaser*

"The NYPD carries out more stops where there are more black and Hispanic residents, even when the history is held constant."

"Blacks and Hispanics are more likely than whites to be stopped within neighborhoods and violated of their life and freedoms, even with our sovereignty for other relevant facts."

"For the period 2004 through 2009, when any law enforcement action was taken following a stop, blacks were 30% more likely to be arrested (as opposed to receiving a summons) than whites, for the same suspected crime."

"For the period 2004 through 2009, after patrolling for suspected crime and precinct characteristics, blacks who were stopped were about 14% more likely—and Hispanics 9% more likely—than whites to be subjected to the use of force."

If these statements and numbers sound familiar, as published by *The Atlantic* in 2013, it's not because you read them in a made-up book. It's not because you saw them on a fictional TV show. It's because **black** people live this reality every day, and it's because countless people of color have had these same experiences whether they are from

New York City, Chicago, Miami, or any other city you can think of.

Excessive force, discrimination, stop-and-frisk, unlawful arrests, killings in the streets, racial profiling, unfair sentencing, harsh punishments—the list goes on. At what point is enough, enough? When can men that look like me feel safe on the streets? History has proven we can't sleep in our homes like Breonna Taylor, we can't play video games with our loved ones like Atatiana Jefferson, and we can't reach for our IDs when asked like Philando Castile.

Don't get me wrong. This ain't a book about police killings or injustices to black people. This ain't a book about pointing fingers and calling racists out. I think we've all heard enough about them in the media, in the news, and in real life. However, this is *my* story, *my* experience, and *my* life as a **black man** and a **black survivor**, who faced real trauma and overcame real obstacles. This is *my* truth. Straight, no chaser.

Life is tough for everyone, for a number of reasons, and no one under the sun is exempt from hurt, grief, or disappointment. For me, life dealt me a cruel hand at a young age, and for a while, it seemed like those emotions were all I knew. Every day was a struggle to get through the next 24 hours. Trouble followed me. Society judged me. Mental and physical abuse consumed me. Pain was a constant "friend." I learned early on how to survive, how to cope, and how to persevere, even when the world seemed to turn its back on me.

As I look back on my journey of hardships and all the challenges I've overcome, I realize how each one prepared me. Every trial equipped me to keep going and inspire the next person to move forward. Every lesson was an opportunity to learn, grow, and mature. Every moment of trauma and defeat shaped me into the man I am today—stronger, wiser, and more resilient.

But it wasn't always like this. I can remember a time of innocence that was cut short. It was a time in my life that I kept silent for many years and buried where I longed for it to stay—in the past. I was just shy of reaching my double digits when I first learned that I was adopted. Imagine taking all of this in at only eight years old. It would be tough for any *adult* to process this, let alone a child.

This was the first of many adversities I would face. I grew up in a toxic environment, in a house that was cold and where "tough love" was more tough than love. It felt like everyone was fighting with *something*. The adults were angry, and the children's behavior reflected that anger. Abuse was frequent, and secrets were swept under the rug, never to be spoken again. Every day presented a new challenge.

I was in the system, trying to claw my way to the top. The system was unforgiving to me; it wasn't fair, and it damn sure wasn't a game.

Surviving the system was a must, but my brutha, if I can do it, so can you...

On November 25th, in the early '80s, on Thanksgiving Day, God saw it fit to put me on this earth one month before Christmas. But as it turns out, I didn't feel like much of a gift to anyone for most of my youth because there was a toxic environment surrounding me at every turn.

I can vividly remember the people, places, and things that shaped my childhood. I remember the neighborhood where we lived. It was rough, so you had to watch your back. Two blocks from our house, there was a big, abandoned lot that people would be ducked off into and, most times, up to no good. It wasn't uncommon to find bullets, human bodies, dead animals, and trash in that lot. My mother, Connie, didn't want us playing or even walking back there, but she would catch us because there were burs in the lot that would stick to our clothes, and if we weren't careful, we would accidentally leave a few on.

Connie was a short-tempered, cold woman who hated noise, which was surprising since she did a lot of yelling. She was a woman of few words, and she stayed in her room in the basement, reading romance novels most of the time. My father, Jeff, was about ten years older than my mother. Jeff's side of the family were slaves from the Deep South, and after his sister was falsely accused of stealing jewelry and hanged, his family migrated to the North for a better life. They were old fashioned, and not a lot of warmth and affection made up their relationship.

My home was often run like a business with very little support and understanding. All the children were raised to respect our elders and to be militant. I remember the weekend that changed my life forever; we were out of school for Spring Break, and the family's energy was different. My sisters were in a good mood, and everybody gathered in the basement to watch TV after breakfast, where Connie's room was. Breakfast that day consisted of cereal with spoiled milk, but I ate and drank it anyway so that I could leave the table. Jeff didn't really like us to watch TV, but that day, my sisters got the chance while he was asleep on the living room floor.

Out of all the children, my biological sister, Trina, was the golden child, so to speak. Connie spoiled her. Sometimes when my mother would get angry, she would tell me she didn't want me and that the only reason I was there was because she wanted my sister. I was a quiet child, more of a loner than the rest of the children, and a bit on the shy side. I didn't talk much, but I observed *everything* that everybody did and took notes. When my sister, Trina, was younger, she hardly ever got in trouble, and the one time I remember her getting slapped, Connie hit her so hard that she fell out of the kitchen chair.

I remember the way our house was set up. There was a two-level stairway, and between each level, you could access the side of the house. I would stay by myself and play in that small area with my cars and toys and never cared to join my family to watch TV downstairs. As long as I was in sight, I enjoyed the freedom of playing alone.

One day, I was on my stoop playing, and I could hear my sisters start asking questions, and then those questions turned into a truth serum. My sisters wanted to know about the family dynamics. This information stopped me in my tracks, as I eavesdropped from upstairs. We found out, from Connie, that my sister, who is two years older than me, and I were both adopted. Like I said, I was only eight years old when I learned this for the first time and tried to process what it meant for my life.

I later learned that when my biological mother was pregnant with me, she had been in court and lost custody of Trina and my older brother. The court deemed her unfit as a mother, and on top of that, she was addicted to partying and alcohol. She didn't want custody of her children anyway, so she made the decision to give up my sister. To this day, I'm not sure what happened to my brother. When I was born, she signed over her parental rights in the hospital, and I went to the family that had taken my sister in. It was understood that the social worker didn't want us to be split up or lost in the system. We were a package deal.

My sister, Trina, ended up asking more questions that day, and we learned that my father was Puerto Rican, who spoke very little English, and that was that. The cards were all out on the table, and now it was time to put the pieces together. Every child wants to feel like they belong, and every child wants to feel loved, so this new information was shocking. Hurtful, even.

Naturally, my reaction was that I wanted to live somewhere else. I didn't like living in that house; I didn't like how I was treated, and somehow, I always knew something was up. I always knew that there were some questions that needed answers. My siblings and I didn't look alike. That was always at the back of my mind, even at a young age. How could we be related when we shared no resemblance? Then, as the information unfolded about our adoptions, it was the confirmation that told me we weren't really connected how a real family should be.

But these answers weren't enough. I needed to know more. I remember sneaking away to my room, in a daze, and just staring into space. My emotions were all over the place, hitting me at once. Anger. Sadness. Confusion. And then I started thinking about my biological mother. *Is she on drugs? Is she even alive? Where is she now? How could a mother just give up her child? Is she coming back to get me when all of this is over?* With all the anger and frustration built up inside of me and no way to release the hurt and confusion, I began to act out. It was a domino effect.

To make matters worse, my parents were old fashioned and were big on hand-me-downs. The new clothes would start with the eldest child, and if the next sibling could fit them, they were handed down to them, and then to the next child, until it got to the youngest. I didn't understand this concept. It wasn't like we were struggling. We could afford newer, nicer clothes, but my parents chose to move clothes and shoes from child to child. Because of this, other kids would make fun of us when we would go outside to play. I was happy when the school implemented uniforms because it took some of the pressure off of us to wear name brand and in-style clothes. By wearing what everybody else had on, at least we only had to focus on shoes.

I remember Jeff working a lot. He had two jobs—one as part of the kitchen staff with the Board of Education, and the other as a porter, working in transit. When he came home from his first job, he'd change clothes and then head out for his second job. He was a man of few words who didn't show affection or open up about anything. If he did open his mouth to speak, it was probably to yell at one of us, or compare us to his co-workers' kids.

He was all about his work and he pushed the males in the house to go to school and learn a trade. At a young age, we learned to work with our hands, and we helped him out with different chores around the house, since he had bad arthritis. I worked on cars, household stuff, you name it. Like I said, everything was ran like a business and not a home. There was no emotional attachment, or any special attention shown, unless we were getting our asses beat.

For some reason, I took the cake with that. Trouble just seemed to linger around me, and it wasn't necessarily my fault but had more to do with the people I hung out with around the neighborhood or at school. They weren't the best examples, and I found myself getting in more and more trouble as I got older. All the children got beatings, but I received the worst of them. Punishments ranged from shadow boxing until my arms were numb, doing hundreds of push-ups until my body gave out, and other cruel and unusual methods.

This was only the beginning of my troubles.

There was a point where I didn't want to go to school. I didn't want to be in the position to act out or be around troublemakers for fear that I would also get in trouble with the school and with my parents. I felt like there was always something going on around me, and for some kids, if they can't find peace at home, they can at least go to school and find it there. For me, I couldn't find peace *anywhere;* that is, until I fell in love with hip hop.

Music, at an early age, was my outlet and lifestyle. I loved hip hop, not just because of the rhymes and beats, but because the music provided an escape for me. Whenever I could get my hands on a tape, I was all over it. I remember Jeff found an old radio, and I ended up fixing it and keeping it. I was happy to finally have something of my own and have something I enjoyed doing. I figured out how to get the Hot 97 radio station, and that was something to look forward to whenever I needed to think or "get away." My only worry was trying not to get the radio taken away because of my behavior.

I would steal cassette tapes from my sister, Trina. She had the latest tapes from DJ Clue and Big Daddy Kane. I was a fan of most of the stuff she listened to. This was around the time that kids would record songs from the radio on to the cassette, so she had the latest music on her tapes. We would go at it whenever she found out I took her tapes, but I couldn't help it. Music was my life and became my muse. It was the only thing, at that point, that I loved and enjoyed.

Sometimes when I would be alone in my room during punishments, I would draw and let out my frustrations that way. But it was mainly the storytelling in hip hop that held my interest. I found myself wanting to know what these guys were saying, so I kept busy by writing down the lyrics to my favorite songs. I would play the music, stop the tape, and then write the words down. Then, I'd rewind the tape, play it again, and then stop it. I would repeat the process until I had the full song written down.

Once a punishment was over, I would be allowed to go back out and hang with my friends. Being the quiet, shy kid, I would play to a certain extent, but it was my friends who did most of the fooling around. So, I was guilty by association, most of the time, and that terrified me because I knew the consequences of my actions. The *only* fear I've ever had in life was of my childhood home and the turmoil it represented. This fear was instilled at a very young age. Every time I got in trouble, I feared going to the house and feared what would happen to me.

At one point, Connie took me to see a therapist, and I was given medication because Connie didn't understand why I was so silent all the time and unengaged with everyone yet still repeatedly in trouble. I would spit the medicine out when she wasn't looking. Even at an early age, I knew that I didn't need to be on medicine, but my teachers insisted, and Connie persisted until I was old enough to refuse it myself.

I remember walking to the neighborhood school each morning. There was a group of us that would meet up and walk together, and the oldest child would watch over everyone else. Once we got to school, that's when the mischief started.

One particular day, I remember my friend got ahold of some matches. We went to the bathroom and played around—anything to get out of learning. Like most schools, the bathrooms weren't the cleanest, and kids had tissue everywhere on the floor and around the sinks. So, as we were playing with the matches, one of the pieces of tissue caught on fire, but because there was so much tissue lying around, the fire started spreading. We tried to put it out, but it became too overwhelming to control.

We decided to run out of the bathroom, but before we could, the alarm systems went off. Eventually, once everything got settled, the principal told the teachers to report the names of students who were in the classroom during the incident and the students who weren't. Of course, I was in the latter group. I thought I had gotten away with it and tried to talk my way out of it, but it didn't work. Connie came to the school and started beating my ass, and then when we got home, it continued. That day, my beatings were taken to another level.

Because of the abuse at home and at school—the teasing about my clothes, about being light-skinned, and about being adopted—my anger continued to build, and I needed to find a release. I wouldn't intentionally aggravate people, but if problems came up, it was hard for me to just ignore a situation and turn the other cheek. So, I did what most children would have done. I fought back. I started getting into fights every day, and it was like a form of therapy. For that moment, it helped me feel better to be able to defend myself, but at the back of my mind, I knew I was hurting others because *I* was hurt.

I remember an incident leading up to the summer; I was a preteen by this time. It involved me and another student, who was climbing on a metal piece of the school jungle gym. I was in line with the other kids, ready to go back into the school when he started running his mouth, provoking me. At that point, I was ready for whatever. I was tired of being picked on, and I didn't care about the consequences. I just wanted to shut him up.

While he was still hanging on the jungle gym, I ran up and grabbed at one of his legs. He started kicking at me, and then I was able to get ahold of both legs. My intention was to pull him down to the ground so I could beat him up, but he lost his grip and ended up falling. His chin hit the metal piece of the jungle gym and the force of it split his chin open.

Of course, I ended up getting suspended and had to stay home for a few days. When I returned to school, I found out that my best friend, Jamel, had been getting picked on by the class bully. Jamel had bad asthma, so I knew he couldn't fight even if he wanted to. As a person who hates seeing others oppressed, it made me angry that this bully was messing with my friend, so not even a full day after I had returned to school from being suspended for fighting, I got into *another* fight so that I could defend my friend.

I ended up walking him home and making sure he was alright, and then I got beat for getting home late. Connie didn't know what had happened, but then when she saw my clothes ripped from the fight, I received a second beating. My mother didn't ask a lot of questions; she just handed out beatings, and I can recall only one time that she actually defended me instead of beating me senselessly.

I would eventually try to run away from home with this same friend with the bad asthma. I spent an afternoon fighting the classroom bully with boxing gloves that Jeff had given me. He was the same boy who I had pulled down off the jungle gym, and he was my mother's friend's son. After beating up the boy, I knew I couldn't go home and face the consequences of my actions, so I convinced Jamel to come with me.

I didn't know where we were going, but I just knew we had to keep walking. I remember it took us hours, since we had to keep stopping and take breaks because of his asthma flareups. Even though I didn't stay away from the house very long, I got home late enough to see Jeff coming home from work, around two in the morning.

That day, I received the worst beating of my life to the point that I blacked out. I was positive my parents knocked the consciousness out of me. I couldn't sit down for a while from the blisters and welts, and I was suspended for the rest of the year for fighting. I ended up missing my own graduation ceremony because of it.

It was a never-ending cycle that I couldn't escape. If I wasn't full-out fighting, I was getting into it with kids. If I wasn't causing trouble at school, I was fighting in the streets. If I wasn't defending my friend, I was trying to defend myself. I felt stuck, like I was in my own personal prison and my own personal hell. I felt alone and like no one understood me.

Many times, I wished I could be taken out of the house and put into a different home.

3 | *Dysfunctional Family*

Connie got involved with a few things happening at my school and maintained a good rapport with the principal and some of the teachers. She was part of the PTA and would babysit some of the teachers' kids. As a child, I was under the impression that my mother didn't work a single day in her life, but I would learn later that she had a job at the post office. After retiring, Connie got into foster care, as a means of income.

For years, she would take in other children that were in foster care, and some of them Connie adopted. There were around 20 to 25 children. But it was weird because it all seemed like an act. Correction: it *was* a front. Whenever we were in public, Connie would pretend we were this loving family who had it all together, but behind closed doors, it was the complete opposite. I guess she did this to show the school staff and to show others that she had it all under control.

Whenever Jeff got home from work, if he got word that I had been acting up in school, he never missed a beating. It was like I was punished twice—first from my mom and then my dad. Connie would tell Jeff ahead of time if I had been acting up, and sometimes, he wouldn't even wait until

I woke up. He would just start beating me while I was asleep with nothing but anger behind his punches.

Jeff was an angry guy in general. He would tell us stories all the time about how he had to walk miles to school when he was younger, and he harbored a lot of resentment for some reason. He mumbled to himself a lot—conversations I couldn't and didn't want to understand. The anger he felt would be taken out on me, and I remember he would use a car radiator hose no bigger than the width of my wrist and the length of my arm, but it brought much pain to me so many times. None of my other sisters and brothers were treated that way or experienced beatings of that magnitude. The mental and physical abuse was just too much. Many times, I remember my sisters running to tell on me if I did something, and then later laughing at me while I received my punishments. To this day, that was something I never understood.

On top of that, the "family" dynamic was crazy. We were the black version of the Brady Bunch. In other words, there were too many mouths to feed. In addition to my sister and me, Connie adopted two other girls and then eventually took their brother in. Then, another girl was adopted, as a baby, like me. The other children in the house were foster children who came and went and the kids she babysat. I remember always sharing a room with one or two people. At any given time, we would come home from school and there would be another kid there, taking up space, and staying at the house.

Sometimes we would see parents come by to pick up the children, but it was mostly how we adjusted to life, seeing people come and go. We just knew this was how it was going to be. This made for a toxic environment and an unhealthy living arrangement with constant mental and physical abuse. The house didn't feel like a home, with love, support, and encouragement. It was just a business with people coming and going and with lots of harbored resentment and anger.

Even with all the kids, my parents already had two children of their own—a girl, Joanne, who was the oldest, and a boy, Jacob. Joanne wasn't home for long, but whenever she was present, she was the only person that gave me attention and concern of any kind. If I wanted something special, most times, she made it happen. For my birthday, one year, she even took me to see *Back to the Future*, when it premiered.

Joanne's bedroom was in the attic, and she had a big waterbed that I liked jumping on. For the most part, she had a good attitude, which was different than her parents. Out of all the children, she would let me come around her friends and hang with them. One year, right before she left for the military, I remember she asked me what kind of sneakers I wanted because she was going to gift me some. I thought the British Knights were dope, and I asked for a pair, not really expecting anything to come of it. That ended up being a highlight for me, because she bought them for me. I wasn't used to people doing nice things for me like that, and I had some shoes that were actually new and in-style. I appreciated that moment because happy moments and happy days were few and far between.

Just as soon as I found a little sunshine, it seemed the storms rolled right in and disrupted everything. A lot of issues were swept under the rug, never to be seen again or talked about. We didn't ear hustle or pay attention to grown folks' business as kids, but one of the things that would later come out was that Jeff had a daughter outside of his marriage to Connie.

As I got older, I realized why Connie was probably so unhappy and angry and why she took her frustrations out on us. Even though it wasn't right, she probably still couldn't process Jeff's infidelity, and seeing his daughter was a constant reminder. Whenever the daughter came over, we assumed it was an aunt and didn't ask questions. It wasn't our business anyway.

Connie was a homebody and didn't have many friends or outlets to release all the hurt and pain she was dealing with. One of her sisters, Laverne, was my favorite aunt and who I wish could have raised me, would come over. My aunt was beautiful inside and out and was the only reason any of the children had birthday parties or experienced family cookouts. We loved going to her house and envied the love and support she showed her daughter, since we never experienced that. I remember that every time Aunt Laverne came around, I felt better.

During Connie's lowest points, she and Aunt Laverne would go on trips together to Las Vegas or Atlantic City, and there were certain things that my mother would hide from us and Jeff, like smoking cigarettes and gambling. She could get away with it because Jeff worked so much, or she would hide out in the basement to do it. But even if he knew what she was doing or if he sensed that the kids were hiding something from him, he still never confronted the issues. He only talked around it in a weird way.

I was in pretty good shape, since Jeff had us doing physical labor at early ages and since I had always been athletic and active, so my mother would send me on runs for her. I remember always going to the store, whether it was just for Bubbalicious gum and Häagen-Dazs, or for full grocery shopping. Even still, my muscular body was no match for that of my parents' biological son, Jacob, who was much scarier and bigger.

He was a monster in his own right and just as toxic as my parents. Jacob got off on terrorizing us. I guess the apple didn't fall too far from the tree with him. He was the complete opposite of his sister, who was kind to me. Jacob played football and was stronger than us, so he would throw his weight around and bully us. Now that I think about it, he was probably insecure about his stuttering problem, so he used violence to make himself feel better. He wanted to be a pretty boy and keep up with the rest of the street dudes, but it came off as fake most of the time. I knew that wasn't how he really was.

Whenever Jacob would babysit the younger kids, he would make us fight each other, and we all dreaded being left alone with him because we knew what was going to happen. He got a kick out of torturing us physically and abusing us verbally, saying things like, "Nobody wanted y'all!"

Even though he messed with all the children, again, I was the magnet for most of the misfortune. I don't know what it was, but I always got the worse of it. Whenever we would play football, Jacob would throw the ball extra hard to me and make me sprain my fingers. If I was told to stay in the house as punishment for something I'd done, he would come in and spit on me or hit me and just do little things when nobody was watching. He was older, so he got away with most of it.

He was someone who got his way most of the time, and if he wanted to dress a certain way or talk a certain way or do something, he was usually able to. The only positive from having him around was when it was time to receive his hand-me-downs. Jacob took good care of his clothes, so most of the stuff he passed on to me looked newer and was still in good condition.

I didn't find much joy in anything or anyone. Birthdays and Christmas was never fun. I was always deprived of gifts because of my bad behavior, and I was usually being punished around those times. I do remember opening up a scarf here and there or pajamas or other things that Jeff found while working in transit. But while the other children opened presents, I just sat back and watched. Holidays, for me, were not the joyous occasions most people can recall from their childhoods.

I hated it, especially because Trina got *everything*. She was spoiled and received all the up-to-date clothes, footwear, and jewelry she wanted. On top of that, she used every chance she got to tell on me whenever she caught me doing something. Years later, when I was in junior high, I learned that she was cutting school, so I used that to blackmail her.

Payback, baby.

4 | *Trouble Don't Last Always, Or Does It?*

As I grew older, I realized school wasn't for me and made the decision to stop attending. I started hanging out with some older dudes from the school, who weren't necessarily the best crowd to hang around, but it was like a family. We would skip school, go buy brew, smoke bud, and just hang out and do what we wanted. Nobody was snitching on anybody, and I enjoyed the freedom and the idea of being "grown up." Nobody could tell me anything.

I was introduced to bud at nine years old and became addicted to the high it gave me, so naturally, I wanted to smoke it all the time. This continued through the years. Then, I started dabbling in selling it so that I could make a little money on the side. This intrigued my older brother, Jacob, who had been trying to get into this lifestyle. I made a hole in my closet and would stash the money I made in there. I would even rob some of the kids from the school, but that didn't last long. The fast life caught up to me and my dope boy ambitions died as quickly as they had started.

One day, while cutting school, I robbed some lame kid from school, and I remember seeing him point at me while he was talking to the principal, but I didn't think nothing of it. Me and my friends ended up driving to Brooklyn and then going to the house of an older dude that we knew. He was a professional car thief and had built his reputation off of it. If there was a particular car that you wanted, he was the one to get it and sell it to you. At the time, there was a new BMW out, with the BBS rims. The man was able to get the BMW, and that's what we sat in as we skipped school.

For my age, I always looked older since I grew facial hair early, so getting liquor from the corner store was never a problem for me. It was my friends who were always caught or denied. I remember, on this particular day, we bought a cheap bottle of alcohol called Old Grand-Dad, and we were sitting around in the BMW, drinking and rolling blunts. I'll never forget that one of my friends wanted to dip the blunts in the liquor. It was hilarious. We were just teenagers, being dumb and playing around.

The dude who had stolen the car was in the driver's seat, and I noticed how he started the car with a screwdriver. He drove us around the block, showing off the BMW, and then we pulled up in the back of the house, near the abandoned lot. The windows were rolled up, and we continued to smoke and hang out. Midway through, the driver got a call from a girl that he wanted to see who lived nearby. As we got to the other side of the backstreets, I kept monitoring the time. Even though I skipped school, I still stayed within the timeframe of the school day so I could at least pretend that I went.

By now, it was a little bit past the time I was supposed to be home, so I was nervous on top of being high, knowing there was no way I could sober up before I made it back home. The older dude with the BMW was talking to his girl. She was leaning into the car, and most of the windows were fogged up. As we were still sitting in the back, blowing and passing, I noticed a police car pull up behind the BMW.

The first thing out of my mouth was, "Oh, shit! The blue and white is behind us!" Panic immediately set in because this was the worst possible time to be pulled over or arrested with the amount of weed and alcohol we had on us, on top of us being underage. Everything just went downhill from there. Without even telling his girl anything, the driver just put his foot on the gas and pulled off. The police took off after us, and all I could think was, *I really did it this time.*

The dude jumped across the lane and started driving on the opposite side of the street, down the backstreets that we knew so well, since we lived in the neighborhood. The chase lasted another five to ten minutes before we ended up losing the police, and then we ditched the car and split up. I headed home, relieved, but being a hustler, I had two beepers and money on me. I was also wearing a chain and a watch and had fronts in my mouth. These were all things that wouldn't have been approved by my parents, so every day, I had to remember to take off everything and hide them in my pockets or in my book bag.

As I was walking towards my block, I saw police cars in front of my house. I noticed my sister, Tiffany, running up, saying, "Ooh, you in trouble! You gon' get arrested!"

I didn't know what the fuck was going on, so I told myself to empty my pockets, but a part of me just gave up. I didn't know what the police were doing at my house or what they wanted, so I just waited to see what was about to happen. I just accepted it.

As soon as I stepped in the front door, Connie started slapping me, and I saw a couple policemen standing around. They began to question me and told me that whatever I had in my pockets, I could give to my mother. As I emptied my pockets, took off my jewelry, and removed my fronts, Connie's slaps turned into punches. I could tell she was the angriest she had ever been with me. For so long, I had told myself that I wanted to be out of the house and sent away, but I never expected to be taken away in a police car.

I was taken to the precinct around four that afternoon, and I remember waiting for hours and hours, until almost four in the morning. I felt a couple of different emotions as I sat there, waiting on the transport to take me to Spofford Juvenile Jail. I felt good because I was finally out of the house I hated so much; I felt nervous because I didn't know what was about to happen; and I felt a little bit worried about what I had just gotten myself into. But I knew, regardless, I wasn't going to allow anybody to step on me or push me around.

Once I got to Spofford, I went through the intake process. I had my clothes taken away, and was strip-searched before and after I took a shower. When I got there, it was early in the morning, so everybody was asleep. I think I stayed up that whole day, because it seemed like as soon as I closed my eyes, it was time to get up. The lights popped on and it was time for the count. All I remember thinking, as I looked around, was that I had been introduced to yet *another* system.

Spofford was set up like a boot camp, except nobody willingly signed up for it. We had ten to fifteen minutes to line up for breakfast each morning, and every meal was timed. I noticed right away that the guards were strict, and across the way, there were girls in the facility, too. It was an adolescent jail, and we were all young prisoners, stuck in a situation we didn't want to be in. I couldn't believe what I was seeing.

The rooms in Spofford had either single or double cells. I happened to be in a double cell with another person. That day, during our late snack, which was cookies and milk, I saw a guy come into our cell and ask my roommate for his cookies. My roommate must've already known what was coming because he had crushed his cookies into his milk and told the guy, "Nah."

Then, the guy turned to look at me and said, "Yo, let me get them cookies."

I just looked at him at first, because I didn't really want to deal with the situation. I knew I wasn't going to let him punk me, so I said, "No, I want my cookies."

That pissed him off, and he started saying some bullshit, which led to more bullshit being said, and I realized right then that I had to make my mark and make a name for myself. It was the only way I would earn my respect.

We ended up fighting in the cell until somebody came and broke us up. The guards made me pack up my belongings, and I was relocated to a dorm that was worse than my previous one. Because I took the first swing, they considered me the aggressor. Once I was moved to the new area, I noticed the guys were a lot bigger than me, but I didn't have any problems, and nobody messed with me.

Between the back and forth with social workers and counselors, I ended up staying in Spofford for a few months, before I went to court. I really didn't understand what was going on, but I never saw Connie, and I found out that she had opened up a case against me so that I would be awarded to the state. In other words, my mother didn't want to be responsible for me any longer. She said she couldn't do anything else with me, so I was sent back to juvenile jail until my next court date.

When the paperwork was finalized, I was sent to Spofford in the Bronx, which was like Riker's Island for teenagers. We rode the bus to Beach Avenue, where we were dropped off to a place called the Beach House. Like its name suggested, it looked like a house, and that image is something I'll never forget it. My name was the third one of six "inmates" called, so I had my cuffs taken off, and one by one, we were admitted into the house.

I took some time to look around as best I could. Right away, I noticed it looked better than the juvenile jail I had come from. This was a more livable, comfortable situation. There was a pool table and an ice hockey table, and it appeared to be more of a group home setting. As I walked towards the window, I looked out and saw one of the counselors. He started flipping out on me and yelling at me.

I was confused and didn't really know what was going on, so I said, "What?" The way I responded must've upset him, so he had one of the correctional officers put the cuffs back on me and basically told me, "You're going back."

Sure enough, I was sent back to the jail. When a social worker interviewed me the next day about what had happened, I was told that looking out the window was considered "attempted AWOL." Obviously, I didn't know the rules, so they brought me back to the Beach House to try again.

During the intake process, I had to take off my sneakers and received some plastic slippers to wear. It was evening by this time, so I had a little snack and then went to bed. When I woke up the next morning, I got up and observed more of what was going on. People were playing around me and doing typical dumb stuff that teenagers do. Once again, I was thrown into an unfamiliar situation with strangers.

I eventually went downstairs and ran into a guy that told me he would help me out. I asked him a few questions about how everything worked, and then it was time for us to go to school, out in Queens. Every morning, we had a routine of eating breakfast, completing our assigned chores, and then going to the private school run by the Beach House agency. The counselors stayed with us the entire time. There were between sixteen and twenty teenagers at any given moment in the house.

I tried my best to stay on the straight and narrow, but trouble found me again. One day, I remember eating breakfast, and one of the female counselors told me I needed a chore assigned to me. One of the guys, who was the "supervisor" over the rest of the teens, wanted me to do the dishes, out of spite. I saw the number of dishes in the sink and told him I wasn't doing it. There were a bunch of pots, pans, and long trays.

The supervisor followed behind me and told me I needed to do the dishes, or the rest of the teenagers wouldn't be able to go anywhere or do anything. I told him, "Well, I guess we just gon' be sitting here."

I walked out and went into the living room area and could hear the other people whispering, saying things like "the new boy doesn't want to listen," and about how I was going to mess up the program because I refused to do the dishes. I didn't care and I wasn't going to comply. I decided to go back up to my room and lay down. Eventually, some counselors found me upstairs and told me it was against the house rules to leave the downstairs area.

The female counselor approached me and told me someone would help me with the dishes, but my mind was still made up. I didn't want to do the dishes, and I wasn't going to. I didn't care if I had help or not. Eventually, she wore me down, and I agreed to help with the dishes. Because I was the new kid, the guy who originally asked me to do them started talking shit to me, on top of being mad that he had to help me with the dishes.

All along, I tried to avoid conflict, but enough was enough. I grabbed a heavy frying pan, and all I remember is swinging it at his face. It ended up busting his head open, and I remember the counselors clearing out the house as they took everyone to school up in Queens. I stayed back and had to wait for the transport to take me back to Spofford for a third time, where I stayed for a few weeks.

When I returned to the house, I saw a bunch of new people, and I realized this was more of an intake house until the counselors figured out where you were going. I'll never forget the vans we rode in, because it looked like we were going to rehab. It was embarrassing.

My stay at the Beach House didn't last long, and I was taken to *another* group home in the Bronx. We had a cool, white teacher who looked more like a biker than an educator. We took trips to the arcades and attended different events. It was four of us to a room usually, and during this time, we would sneak away to smoke weed or cigarettes.

At the home, we received an allowance, but we weren't allowed to buy tobacco with it, so we would sneak around and get our fixes in other ways. One day, we decided to sneak out to the store, and we took a cue from the movies. We took some bed sheets and tied them together and hung them out of the window to get close enough to the ground so a friend and I could escape from a second-story window.

When we returned, the sheets were taken out of the window, the lights were off, and the teens were all gathered around in the rec room. We looked at each other and told ourselves we weren't going back in there, so we snuck off to the Bronx and got into a little trouble for a few days. Eventually, we were picked up by truant police on the street—we were considered AWOL. We were taken back to our group home, but it was too late. I had gotten my taste of freedom and I chased it. I wanted to be on my own and do my own thing.

My friend got into selling drugs, and to make my own money, I helped him out for a little while before I was shipped off to another group home in Westchester. At that point, I didn't know whether I was coming or going. This was another adjustment I had to make, but I was disgusted by what my life had become. Thankfully, I ended up getting linked with a female social worker who actually cared and who I took a liking to. I could tell she wanted to help me, and I appreciated it.

The social worker encouraged me to get involved in sports when she heard that I was active and could run fast. I ended up doing well in relay racing, sprinting, and hurdles, and most of my awards and medals were for first place. Sports were a good distraction for me at fifteen. Because of it, my popularity soared, and opportunities opened up for me. But this was short-lived. I still felt lonely, and mischief still came knocking at my door.

During these times of loneliness, readjustment, and not feeling wanted, I realized I didn't want this for my life. I didn't want to be told what to do, how to act, when to eat, and how to behave by people who didn't have it together themselves. I wanted more for my life, no matter the labels that were slapped on me or the odds that were thrown against me. People would tell me all the time in the group homes that I would be dead before the age of 21, and the fact that they counted me out was crazy. Who tells a kid that?

I was determined to make it out of the system, one way or another, but I did not realize I would fall into the same trap, years after my release from the group home at the age of 19. On January 4, 2011, I was once again shipped off and placed in a *real* jail to start an eleven-and-a-half-year sentence, and I came out October 24, 2020, a changed man.

I experienced two cases where my decision was set to go to trial. I remember being faced in both courtrooms where the officers' smiles said to me, "We're looking to do a nigger in." There I was, defending my life as a negro man against the racism of the system. Only the true offenders wore robes and badges in disguise of their true selves, as if they are the cowboys and we are the Indians. The watchdogs with the badges of the system still ran their own set of rules. I must have run into one that night—a racist, scary, dangerous, adrenaline-junky cowboy cop with a dog. Except this Indian wasn't unarmed against this tyrant that night.

But we all know how this ends, and my survival depended on it.

However, he had different plans regardless of what I had or didn't have. I just couldn't allow a person to be in control of my destiny. But it was almost too late. I knew I had an angel watching over me even though I woke up handcuffed to a hospital bed. Like my case and most other cases, people automatically side with the "uniform." If you have a badge and a gun, you can pretty much get away with anything. With any other job, you have to leave your problems at home and be on your best behavior, so to speak. With some police officers, they bring their problems to work and don't care who they disrespect or hurt in the process. They don't care how their toxicity and negativity affects others.

They just so happen to have jobs where they can do a lot of damage, especially when the individual has no moral compass, and it's been proven that they have done a lot of damage time and time again. Just look at the body count of mistreatments, injustices, and wrongful killings towards civilians. Even if it's just ONE person that they do wrong, their actions affect an entire family, and that's one person too many. But still, they don't give a fuck, so we're left to play the game. We're left to play by their "rules."

I'm disgusted by the system, and I know I ain't the only one. Some of these officers push your buttons so you can break your character and they can look at you and say, "Hey, look at this black man!" They throw around the word "nigga" and other racist slurs and jokes, and laugh about it to your faces, knowing they have whatever power they think they have. They label and stigmatize black men, women, and children incorrectly, disrespect us, and treat us inhumane, with the understanding that we won't fight back. And if we *do* fight back, we either end up dead or in jail.

But they'll never admit it and they'll never see the wrongdoing on their end. I can attest to being caught up and cornered with some coward shit. I'll give you some words and you do the math: racial profiling, illegal search, severe dog bite, and an eleven-and-a-half-year sentence.

Sound familiar? Yeah, well, it happened to me, just like the next man.

No matter if we're innocent or not, we're a target for certain men in blue. I just happened to have a handgun on me, so it didn't take much thought to have me thrown into prison. The same people who swear by "protecting" and "serving" added me to their list of black men who they thought they could take advantage of, and today, I'm still trying to dust myself off from that day.

6 | *Hurt People Hurt People*

A topic that a lot of people don't discuss or think about is the trauma that individuals endure after "graduating" from the system, whether it's jail, a group home, or any other toxic environment. How can someone be the same person after witnessing violence or going through different situations meant to break you? It's impossible to have the same outlook on life and people.

Those experiences cause you to take a step back and evaluate everything with a more discerning eye. You try to figure out if a person's intentions are good or bad, and then you try to avoid the situation, if possible. But we all know trouble still finds you, whether you want it to or not.

As the saying goes, "hurt people hurt people," and no truer words have ever been spoken. It may not be a person's intention to hurt someone else, but it happens, especially if self-healing hasn't taken place. This was important for me. I didn't want to be out there, creating lasting memories with "temporary people" or people not meant to stay in my life beyond a season. I didn't want to hurt people because I knew I would hurt people if I had not healed.

So, I had to go back and address certain wounds and try to remove the labels from my life that I no longer wanted to carry around. I had to get rid of the labels that were self-imposed or placed on me by toxic people. I had to create my own memories and my own peace. I found myself asking, *Who am I? Who is Jermaine?* Finding my true identity was my first plan of action.

I had to embrace the fact that I was different in every sense. I noticed the negative labels that were placed on me and went into survival mode by overprotecting and guarding myself from the attacks that would inflict more pain.

Romantic relationships were a struggle for me, naturally. It wasn't that I didn't want to have a woman to spend time with or a friend to kick it with, but most times, I could recognize early on if it would work out or not. I was and still am a good reader of a person's aura, and I'm very much into the astrological and spiritual world. A lot of women I dated in the past were great women who were beautiful and special but just not right for *me*.

I knew that in order to have a successful relationship, friendship, or partnership of any kind with longevity, healing had to take place before anything else. A lot of people, bruthas especially, won't admit that, but it's something I wanted to do for myself. Without healing or some form of therapy and release, you remain rooted in the past hurts that keep you bound. Who wants to walk around with all that baggage?

That "old person" can and will take over the new you if you allow it, but because I recognized this pattern, that was something I worked on. If I saw a relationship or friendship going left, I took the higher road and backed out of those situations. It may have hurt to do it in that moment, but looking back, I have no regrets. Everything worked out in the end. I know that some people come into your life for chapters, and just like a book, when it's over, it's over. And that's okay.

Not everyone gets into my heart. That's a special place where entry is earned, not given. The environment for bruthas like me, growing up, deprived us of that foundation to stand on, which is crucial to the survival of everyday life. Operating like this was a sort of defense mechanism and a way to protect my energy and peace. For so long, I had been hurt or abused by others, and systems had controlled me in some form. But that wasn't what I wanted for my life, so now, I take every opportunity to control my own destiny and to create my own forms of self-fulfillment and happiness because I realize that no one else will. No one else can have that power over me anymore.

Originally, I was never part of the modern world. However, I observed it. Making judgments about people was never my style, but I don't accept the shit talking or oppression that came from those "modern" people. No one gets a pass. I never cried about the abuse I went through or how I was beaten and treated unfairly or the discrimination I faced for no reason.

Going through the flow of changes that come with uncomfortable situations and living conditions would slow me down a little, but it didn't stop me. Sometimes, finding myself lost in my pain and suffering led me to isolate myself, to roll up blunts and pop some bottles until I passed out. Either way, being stuck deep in my thoughts would still leave me burnt-out.

Memories sometimes have a mind of their own, and somehow, I'm brought back to when I was little. I realize now that my experiences were not about my purpose, because my purpose was and is so much greater than I understood. You create your own reality with your thoughts, negative or positive.

That was another lesson I learned: surviving the system while you're in it is one thing, but surviving the aftermath of it is a whole different ball game. Sadly, only a few survive. With the enforcement of the system, most people don't escape from the traps and the tricks and the trenches, let alone leave the system intact. Only a handful of them go on to lead healthy and productive lives.

There are plenty of people from my group home and my past who I've heard of who passed away from an overdose or suicide, so I consider myself one of the blessed ones. I'm one of the few who made it out and lived to tell my story. This mission is one I don't take lightly. So many people are left to fix the pieces of their broken lives caused by other broken people and that ain't fair.

Not many people are willing to see that destructive and abusive side of the system and the people it creates mentally and emotionally. But for me, growth was inevitable, and if it doesn't add to my progress or peace, it has to go. Living with a victim mentality doesn't suit me. I just let my past experiences prepare me for what's next. I learned that needing someone to feel whole was just an illusion and not the reality.

I **can't** remain silent.

Usually, when you serve a certain amount of time in jail, you're given the choice to seek professional counseling or therapy of some sort after your release. It's a way to evaluate your mental capacity, and to combat any negative outcomes of what you went through. Few people benefit from this or even take the opportunity. I'll be the first to admit that my saving graces didn't come from a therapist wearing nice clothes and holding a pen and notepad. I found refuge in something totally different—cooking.

My passion for cooking started while I was growing up in the group home, but really, I had picked up on a few things while watching Connie. Over time, cooking turned from something I did to survive into something therapeutic for me. There was just something about mixing the different ingredients, adding in the flavors, and watching something I created come to life. Not to mention, every woman loves a brutha who can cook, so it got me brownie points over the years in relationships.

In those moments, I know I'm in control, and I'm turning something so simple into little masterpieces on the plates—or at least I'd like to think so. Your boy can still throw down, too, and cooking continues to be a go-to passion that calms and centers me. In many ways, it's an art form.

Music continued to be something that helped me to escape my reality as I got older, whether I was making it or listening to it. As it is for most people, it became one of my saving graces then and is the same now.

Therapy works for some people and may not work for others. It's best to figure out what speaks to your situation on how you obtain peace. This can be through music, cooking, drawing, writing, prayer, or whatever best fits your needs. Just remember to do what's best for *you* to heal and move forward. REAL TALK!

When my son was born, it was unexpected, but I went into provider mode right away. It doesn't matter if you have everything you think you need, or have nothing at all, the baby is coming regardless, and it didn't ask to be here. So, what are you going to do? You have two options: fold under pressure or step up. That first choice never even crossed my mind.

Knowing my own upbringing, which lacked love, guidance, and support, I wanted to do things differently. I knew I had to be the father and representation of love that I never received as a child. I wanted to protect, guide, and teach my seed the right and wrong ways. I didn't want to be responsible for creating or raising another helpless and broken soul, but someone who could stand on his own two feet when the time came.

Let me just say; parenting is hard, and co-parenting is hard, as well. Anybody with children can tell you that, and it's a lot harder behind bars or when you're not given the opportunity to see your children as often as you would like. Parenting forces you to grow up in ways you never thought you could, and "making ways out of no way" takes on a whole new meaning.

I wasn't a perfect father, and no one is. We all make mistakes. But I was a father who loved and nurtured. I was a father who TRIED and showed up as best he could. I was a father who wanted to be there, no matter what the circumstances presented.

Now, as I look back, I take pride in the different decisions I made in my parenting because it came from a good place and a place of love. It allowed me to give my children the freedom of expression, which is something I didn't have growing up.

9 | *A Place I'll Never Forget*

There aren't too many places on earth that are worse than jail, and I can promise you that. For over 10 years, I sat behind those infamous bars, wishing I could turn back the hands of time just to right a wrong or fix what I had messed up.

Jail is a hostile and unforgettable environment. It's a place I wouldn't wish on my greatest enemy, no matter how much rappers glorify it like it's a badge of honor. I hated it. I was determined to survive, with the promise to myself that I'd never find myself back there again.

Don't let the TV shows fool you. There was nothing funny, glamorous, or cool about spending time behind bars. The showers were dirty, and if you didn't watch your back, the inmate across from you could do you dirty. I knew this place wasn't for me. I had to always be on point and watch my back, especially whenever I walked in the hallways or in the yard. I wasn't trying to get cut, which was a sport behind those walls. Anybody could get it, and *everybody* was a target.

I still remember the yelling between correctional officers and inmates, the mice, and the filth. I still remember the sneak thieves and those who were willing to do anything to catch you slipping. The food was laughable and void of both nutrition and taste. The only thing that kept me motivated was seeing pictures of my son. This kept me going.

I still remember the drugs, the gambling, and the gangs. Yep, even locked up, those things existed. People were ruthless and heartless, and at any given moment, you could become a pawn in another inmate or officer's game. People were killed or harmed every day by staff or their fellow inmates. It's a miracle anyone makes it out untouched.

Jail was segregated. Honestly, it didn't surprise me. We were all inmates, but we still saw color and went where we fit in. We went where we felt the safest and were "accepted," if you even want to call it that. Like any setting, you had your blacks on one side, your whites on another side, and the Hispanics and other races in another area. Cliques and gangs provided a certain level of protection, but trusting anyone was like gambling. You really couldn't trust anybody as far as you could throw 'em.

I still remember the looks and behaviors from racist correctional officers. They didn't care about what went on as long as they received a paycheck. I was just another number to them, another statistic. Their attitudes were serious, direct, and oppressive. Jail was oppressive, and in many ways, it was another form of slavery. Imagine that—shackled men being told what to do, what to eat, and where to go.

I witnessed the unexpected. I experienced a world that is unknown to so many, but it's a place I'll never forget. Because of it, I experienced a transformation while in the "lion's den" that changed my life forever.

As I close out my life experiences, I want you to take these words to heart and to understand that your life has purpose and meaning. Some of us get the shorter end of the stick and have to try to survive a little bit more than the next person, but it's all for the greater good. It's up to you, and what *you* want to do, that will make the difference. Will you give in and die? Or will you pick yourself up and move forward?

Bruthas and sistas, be encouraged as we continue to fight and continue to rise. Make every opportunity in your life count, even if trouble comes or hardships try to threaten your peace. Never give up or give in to your circumstances, and remember—things will always get better.

I look at the man in the mirror every day with gratitude and excitement for whatever life has in store for me. Regardless of what it may be, I know it'll be good because when you give out good energy, you attract it in return. When you compare my life from then, as a broken and abused child, to now, a man who has overcome a *lot* and climbed out of the trenches, there ain't much you can say other than **I did it**—I survived the system.

I don't just call myself the "King of Adversity" for no reason. I have been through it all, and I have the physical scars, experiences, and memories to prove it. The most important thing is that I made it out, and I'm blessed that I don't look like the villain that the world and my circumstances tried to turn me into.

"Love is patient, love is kind. It does not envy, it does not boast, it is not proud. It is not rude, it is not self-seeking, it is not easily angered, it keeps no record of wrongs."

-Corinthians 13:4